Tea Under the Palms

Tea Under the Palms

LADY PATRICIA FARMER

BEAUFORT BOOKS

NEW YORK

Those of you who have read my previous books know that my quest for excellence and everything fabulous began the day I visited New York's famed Plaza Hotel when I was seven years old. On that very special occasion, my mother introduced me to the ritual of afternoon tea at The Palm Court. Sitting on the velvety banquette, feeling very grown up as I sipped and nibbled and looked up at actual palm trees—indoors—was a truly magical experience.

Now, I am fortunate enough to live at The Plaza and enjoy that same beautiful tea service any time I like.

It's still magical.

—Patty

CONTENTS

Tea Under the Palms

CHAPTER 1

TEA STORY
Beginnings

Tea is one of the world's oldest beverages, dating back to China in 2737 BC. After water, it remains the most popular drink in the world. In 141 BC, Emperor Jing of Han was ceremoniously buried in a box along with a variety of treasures he might enjoy in the afterlife. Prominent among them was an urn filled with his preferred tea leaves. In 350 AD, the Erh-Ya, the oldest surviving Chinese dictionary, included an extensive citation on tea. Early Taoists firmly believed it increased the possibility of immortality, and by the fifth century, the aromatic beverage was widely understood to have medicinal properties.

But it wasn't until the advent of the Tang dynasty (618-907 AD) that tea was lauded as much for its pleasant flavor as its healing properties. The first known book on tea—written between 760 and 762 AD by Lu Yu—appeared some 1,500 years into its history and expounded on cultivation techniques and preparation. And it would take until the Sung dynasty (960-1280 AD) for the beverage to evolve to become the center of a social and spiritual ritual in which the cultured and wealthy indulged in dedicated teahouses.

Tea next took hold in Portugal in the mid-1500s, thanks to Jesuit missionaries who traveled to China and wrote home about the miraculous beverage. In journals, Father Matteo Ricci suggested that the preparation of tea enhanced longevity and encouraged energy, and Father Álvaro Semedo described the customs associated with the Chinese tea ceremony.

Surprisingly, tea surfaced in France several decades before overtaking England. Aristocrats in Paris, including Louis XIV and his wife, Queen Marie Antoinette, were ardent tea fanciers as early as 1636 (solving the mystery of what her subjects were supposed to drink with their cake). The Sun King may or may not have savored its taste, but he did hope it would alleviate his gout and strengthen his heart. Madame de Sévigné, who chronicled the activities of Louis and his court, mentioned tea often in her letters and journals, noting in particular the curious custom of one Madame de la Sablière, who made fashionable the habit of adding milk to the beverage. Once this tradition reached England, they quickly adopted what they referred to as the elegant *French touch*. Cardinal

Mazarin, one of King Louis's most trusted advisors, had a veritable addiction to the stuff, consuming at least twelve cups a day.

As popular as it was amongst the aristocracy, tea never really trickled down to the common folk of France; consequently, its consumption took a nosedive after the French Revolution in 1789. It would be fifty years before it would become fashionable again, and by that time, it would be the French copying the English.

In the 1650s, tea was still a novelty in England, thought of mainly as a cure-all. It wasn't until 1662, when King Charles II married the Portuguese princess Catherine of Braganza and a crate of the stuff was included in her dowry, that tea began to hold its own with wine, ale, and spirits. (It's been suggested that the value of those matrimonial tea leaves, which included Bombay and Tangier varieties, was enough to wipe out a substantial portion of the royal debt.) Also included in that dowry—and even more valuable—was permission for the British to use Portuguese-controlled ports in Asia, Africa, and the Americas, thus giving them their first direct access to the tea trade. Under Charles II's reign, the East India Company grew into one of the largest and most important trading conglomerates in the world.

It was during this period that Western traders introduced opium to the Chinese in exchange for their prized tea leaves, ultimately setting off an "opium war" between China and Britain. Fearful that the influx of precious tea would be disrupted, the East India Company set out to establish its own tea plantations in colonial India. There was just one problem: they had neither the seeds nor the know-how to begin, and China wasn't about to reveal secrets it had been protecting for a thousand years. Undaunted, the British traders recruited a Scottish botanist named Robert Fortune to infiltrate China and come back with the knowledge they needed. It was a dangerous mission—punishable by death if he were to be caught. Fortune shaved his head, adopted the regional mode of dress, and spent the years from 1843 to 1851 traversing the Far East, posing as a wealthy Chinese merchant. He managed to gain access to numerous tea farms and learn their techniques for planting, roasting, and drying the crop. He also amassed a stash of more than 10,000 saplings and seeds.

Fortune's triumph precipitated China's downfall within the industry. In the 1850s, India's tea production outstripped China's, and Darjeeling, a city high in the Himalayas, perfected what is still thought of as the champagne of teas, possessing a fruity delicacy that reminds many of, well . . . champagne. (And, like champagne and its official region, no tea may be labeled "Darjeeling" unless it is grown in that particular district of India.) Only in the last few decades has China has regained its position as the world's largest tea producer.

Let's return for a moment to the mid-1600s, and Catherine of Braganza. As Charles II's queen, she never hid her great fondness for tea, partaking of its warmth publicly and often, and the nation followed her lead. First the aristocracy and ultimately the working classes made it more popular than coffee and even whiskey. Catherine is also credited with refining the etiquette of the English table. Prior to her arrival, the English, even the royals, ate primarily with their hands. Queen Catherine maintained the Portuguese custom of using a knife and fork, and it quickly caught on in the royal palaces and eventually filtered to the masses. She also introduced music as entertainment during her elegant parties as well as the very first opera ever to be heard in England. Last but not least—particularly in a book about teatime—Catherine brought orange marmalade to England (lest you thought this British staple was homegrown). Believe it or not, she made it herself and enjoyed giving it to friends.

In 1706, Thomas Twining sensed an opportunity. He purchased Tom's Coffee House at 216 Strand Street in London and turned it into a more gracious venue. It was the first shop to offer fine-quality dry tea as well as coffee. And that wasn't the only difference between his shop and the rest. Because tea, with its claims of health and medicinal benefits, had a more decorous reputation, ladies could now venture in to enjoy a cup of the rich brew without fear of bruising their reputations. Over the ensuing decades, many notable customers took respite there, including Jane Austen and William Hogarth. Twining eventually expanded into a neighboring building and redubbed the larger establishment the Golden Lyon. The shop exists to this day and holds the title of oldest tea shop in London. I strongly recommend a visit for tea and a stroll through the attached museum and shop.

At the turn of the eighteenth century, Queen Anne abandoned her daily breakfast drink of ale in favor of tea, solidifying it as the national beverage. The fashion for adding sugar only enhanced its popularity among the upper classes. Sugar was a luxury most could not afford.

Afternoon or "low" tea developed into a common ritual in the mid-1840s, when Anna Maria, the seventh Duchess of Bedford and one of Queen Victoria's ladies-in-waiting, could no longer bear the "sinking feeling" she experienced during the long period between breakfast and dinner. She began ordering a light mid-afternoon snack, accompanied by a pot of tea, to be delivered to her boudoir at around four o'clock. She soon invited friends to share this small repast while catching up on the day's gossip, and the tradition of at-home tea was born.

The afternoon ritual quickly caught on as an occasion to socialize and commonly took place in outdoor gardens in temperate weather. The middle classes found that "tea parties" were an inexpensive way to entertain and began inviting their friends over for a "cuppa." Not wanting to miss out on the action, dining establishments set aside specific rooms for the gatherings.

Bars and pubs had long been the meeting place of choice for groups of friends, but the rise of the British temperance movement in the 1830s forced people to develop new tastes and diversions. Enter coffee houses, establishments which, though they sound tame enough, tended to be as rowdy as the pubs, were frequented exclusively by men, and were filled with smoke and noise.

Tea rooms soon popped up all over England and the United States—which was experiencing a temperance movement of its own—and it became acceptable for women to socialize without male escorts. It was over tea and sandwiches in these shops that conversations among women turned from gossip and fashion to politics and equal rights, and the Suffragette movement was born.

While it never quite took hold in North America, the custom of taking

afternoon tea became the norm in British society, and the art of hosting a tea party was made part of the curriculum at ladies colleges, along with how to iron a shirt, boil an egg, supervise household staff, and other "women's duties." Employers began to offer tea breaks at mid-morning—"the elevens"—and mid-afternoon.

If there's a low tea, there must be a high, but their respective definitions are a little counterintuitive. As noted, low tea tends to be offered at around four o'clock and typically includes a sampling of delicate sweets and savories—tiny crustless sandwiches, scones, miniature pastries and cakes, and, of course, a pot of tea. It tends to be the province of the leisure classes. High tea, which is sometimes misunderstood as something posh or refined, is actually quite the opposite. During the Industrial Revolution (mid-1700s to mid-1800s), people of all ages worked long, arduous shifts. Knowing that tea functioned as a stimulant, canny employers began offering "high tea"—which included a rather substantial meal—between five and seven o'clock, to keep their workers alert and productive well into the evening.

So how did these rituals get their confusing names? The answer is that the distinction between "low" and "high" relates not to class but to seating. Low tea is traditionally served on low, comfortable chairs or sofas in a drawing room. High tea tends to be served at a table surrounded by high stools or chairs.

To be sure, the customs surrounding tea have changed over time as our work and leisure activities have evolved. High tea has mainly fallen out of vogue, but what is now known simply as afternoon tea has never been more popular.

Harvesting Tea

What, exactly, *is* the exotic, delightful beverage to which this book is devoted?

Tea is produced from the tiny white petals and bright green, leathery, shiny leaves of the shrub known as *Camellia Sinensis*. It thrives only in tropical and semi-tropical climates with sandy, slightly rocky soil, preferably on hillsides for

easy drainage. A tea's variety is determined by how these leaves are processed.

Tea is harvested by hand because only the tender new leaves, buds, and stems at the tops of the plants can be used. Since the earliest days in China, tea pluckers have mainly been women because of their diminutive stature and delicate touch. What's more, these workers have traditionally been forbidden to eat certain foods, such as fish, pungent meats, and spices, lest their breath affect the delicate leaves.

The small cluster of usable leaves is known as "the flush," and is the basis of tea production. If left alone, the plants would grow to fifty feet or more, but growers work hard to suspend their growth with sedulous pruning, and harvests are undertaken twice a year.

There are four primary tea types: black, green, oolong, and white, but surprisingly, they all come from the same tea plant. Each variety acquires its particular attributes during processing, which is done using one of two methods: Orthodox or Cut-Tear-Curl (CTC). Orthodox tea processing is done mainly by hand, while CTC is accomplished by machine. Each step is rigidly controlled, as many variables can alter the entire flavor.

Preparing the Leaves

Essential differences at every stage of the process determine the variety and properties of the final product.

○ Growing and Harvesting: These two steps are grouped, and while this is an obvious first step, growing conditions have an enormous impact on the finished tea flavor. Tea plants grow best in warm areas with heavy rainfall and, just as in the production of wine, changes in climate or soil can dramatically alter the properties of a particular harvest. A prime example is Japanese green tea. Planters typically shade the plants with coverings to encourage more chlorophyll and theanine production. Those growers who choose not to shade their plants produce a very different tasting tea. The method of harvesting is another way of creating variations in taste. Premium tea is harvested by hand to help preserve its natural sweetness. Mass-produced varieties, on the other hand, are harvested by machine and the difference in flavor can be pronounced. When steeped, machine-chopped tea releases the full extent of its flavors quickly, while hand-picked leaves require longer to release their richness.

○ Withering: Because the tea plant's leaves are waxy and thick, they must be softened or "withered" to make them pliable. Toward this end, they are spread on tables or mats in climate-controlled rooms and rotated periodically for optimal airflow. This process reduces the moisture content of each small leaf by half.

○ Bruising: At this step, the leaves are crushed, rolled, and twisted to break down their cells and make them receptive to oxidation. The particular way in which this is done affects the type of tea that is

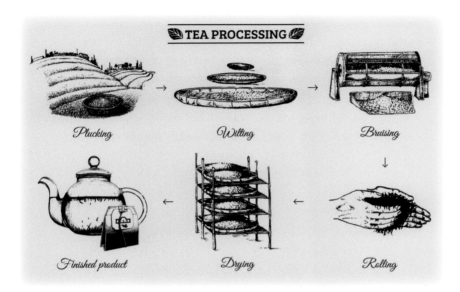

TEA PROCESSING

Plucking → **Wilting** → **Bruising** ↓

Finished product ← **Drying** ← **Rolling**

produced in the end.

○ Oxidizing: Here, the leaves intended for black or oolong teas are again laid out on mats and left to oxidize, turning brown, much like a banana left in the open air. Again, heat and humidity are carefully monitored. (Green teas forgo this aspect of the process entirely, thus their color.)

○ Fixing: Heat is required at this stage to end the oxidation process and "fix" the leaves. This step is sometimes referred to as the *kill green* process—a misnomer as it preserves whatever green hue is left in the leaf at this point.

○ Drying: Finally, the leaves are thoroughly dried to remove any remaining moisture. The choice of drying method can change the taste. Charcoal roasting adds a smoky, rich flavor. Leaves meant for white tea require a gentler hand and are typically sun-baked or slow-baked. After drying, the tea is ready to be sorted, packaged, shipped, and enjoyed.

Varieties of Tea

Now, the leaves have graduated to become a specific tea.

○ Black tea is the most universally recognized and requested tea in the world and makes up seventy-five percent of the market. English Breakfast and Earl Grey are two common brands of black tea, which can be identified by its reddish-brown color and bold face-forward taste.

○ Green tea is exactly that—green or greenish yellow—and tastes as it looks: very light and grassy.

○ Oolong tea falls somewhere between green and black teas in appearance and taste. Because it has been only partially oxidized, it never attains the striking darkness and richness of black tea, but it is more substantial than green.

○ White tea is rare because its leaves can be picked on only two days of the year (before the plant's buds have fully bloomed). White tea has a uniquely delicate and smooth flavor. Not subjected to smoking, drying, or rolling, it contains the highest level of antioxidants and is one of the purest teas. There was a time when white tea was reserved strictly for Chinese nobility and never exported. Today, it is more widely available.

Tea enthusiasts claim that the best tea is loose leaf. This actually makes sense, because the truest flavor and most nutrients come forth when the leaves have enough space to expand and uncurl as the water circulates around them. Premium leaves tend to be sold in a loose-leaf format, while teabags—which confine their content so it can't be steeped as effectively—contain broken leaf bits and dust. The upside of tea bags is their convenience, widespread availability, and relatively low cost.

CHAPTER 2

SPILLING THE TEA
Preparation of the perfect service

Today, afternoon tea is a posh social event typically served between three and five o'clock, usually in a tea salon or designated room in a restaurant. Because of its inherent sense of festivity, afternoon tea is often the basis of a celebration, such as a bridal or baby shower or birthday. It provides an unparalleled opportunity for connection, gossip, and fun.

In earlier times (and among the upper classes), while servants were expected to prepare breakfast, lunch, and dinner, tea was another matter entirely. Once the tea service had been delivered to the room, the hostess would do the honors, occasionally aided by a friend or relative.

A proper tea service would include:

○ A pot of hot water
○ A container of loose tea
○ A tea strainer
○ Milk and sugar cubes
○ A teapot of the proper size for the gathering
○ Teacups and saucers
○ Marmalades, lemon curd, and seasonal preserves
○ A light repast presented on a succession of tiered plates on a wooden stand

All of these items would be placed on a sideboard or table. At the time of service, the hostess would ask each guest about her preferences as to tea strength and milk or sugar. Milk was typically added *after* the tea was poured. (This was meant to confirm the freshness of the milk and high quality of the china; if milk were added first, it might imply that the china was inferior and in danger of cracking.) Because tea tends to cool quickly, each cup would be passed to the guest as it was poured.

Eventually, elegant silver tea services, complete with ornate teapot, creamer, and sugar bowl, became the norm.

The etiquette and traditions associated with afternoon tea have evolved over the years, but the tiered trays remain a signature of the ritual. They represent the

three distinct courses of the service (some say four, including the tea itself as a course of its own). Guests are expected to start with the lowest tray, which holds scones, small muffins, or similar bakery items wrapped in a linen napkin to maintain their just-baked warmth. A signature staple of the service to this day, scones are meant to be gently split horizontally for consumption—never cut with a knife as that tends to ruin their texture. Once split, bite-size pieces may be broken off and dolloped with a bit jam or cream from one's own plate, then eaten immediately. Never, *ever* wash down your bite with tea.

The second course, found on the middle tray, consists of tea or finger sandwiches with their crusts cut off, apportioned into little triangles so they may be consumed in just a few bites. Classic fillings include thinly sliced cucumber, salmon, egg salad, and beef with horseradish. The bread may be white or brown, but it must be soft. I've been told that canny hostesses freeze their bread beforehand so that it can be sliced more cleanly. Guests are expected to consume a maximum of two sandwiches of each variety, so please don't scarf down all the salmon sandwiches before the rest of us can partake.

The top-tier and final course (and my own favorite) consists of sweets. It's here that the pastry chefs have an opportunity to display their creativity. Petit fours, tarts, and miniature éclairs are *de rigueur*, and the prettier the better.

Limited utensils are required at tea—they are called *finger* sandwiches, after all—but keep in mind that only three fingers should be used to eat these dainty bites, never five. You should find a small butter knife to the right of your plate to spread the jam and clotted cream over the pastries, and a teaspoon on your saucer or to the right of your knife. The small spoons accompanying the pots of preserves and cream are for the purpose of getting those extras from their pots to your plate. Never use the preserve spoon in the cream or vice versa; to each its own.

One last admonition: No matter how hungry you are or how enticing the spread, avoid over-filling your plate. Select just two items at a time, enjoy them, and then go back for a refill.

Myka Meier, founder of the internationally renowned Beaumont Etiquette and co-founder of The Plaza Hotel's Finishing Program in New York City, encapsulates the tea experience beautifully. "The perfect service doesn't have to be complicated. It can be as simple or as extravagant as you'd like."

CHAPTER 3

STRICTLY SPEAKING
Etiquette

tiquette guru Myka Meier goes on to explain, "If presented in all its glory, afternoon tea—or just *tea*, as Her Majesty the Queen refers to it—can be an exceptional experience; that is, if etiquette and good manners are observed. Etiquette is simply about being kind, respectful, and considerate to everyone, first and foremost."

While customs of behavior may have changed somewhat since Victorian times, the basics of good manners remain the same and can actually be enjoyable to follow as they contribute to a graceful and gracious experience.

Upon arriving at a tea party—nowadays, typically in a restaurant or tearoom—the first step is to greet your hostess warmly. Once seated, your purse goes on your lap or behind your back against your chair—never on the floor or hung by its strap. And do we need to mention that phones should never be seen or (for heaven's sake!) heard? For that matter, keep all personal items off the table.

Next comes the issue of the napkin, which you should find to the left of your place setting, folded so that the closed edge faces out. You probably know that you should immediately unfold it and place it in your lap, but there is more to know. If you need to leave the table for a few moments, your napkin should be laid neatly on your chair until you return. And when it's time to leave the party, it should be refolded carefully and left it where you found it—at the left of your place setting.

Always hold your teacup by its handle. If the cup is designed in such a way that your finger will not fit through, hold the handle carefully with your thumb on one side and two fingers on the other, and position it so that the handle is in the "four o'clock" position.

Teacups with handles have been around only about a hundred years, so it's possible (though unlikely) that you'll encounter a handleless cup. If so, the proper way to hold it is to place your thumb at the six o'clock position and your index and middle fingers at the twelve o'clock position, and, if necessary for balance, subtly tilt your pinkie up. (The handleless teacup has been around since 620 AD, when China first popularized the beverage. Today, you're more likely to find it in a Chinese restaurant than at a formal tea.)

Sadly, teabags have found their way into some tea parties (I've experienced this firsthand), so you might as well learn the proper way to handle them in public. First and foremost, do not dunk the teabag in and out of your cup to speed up the steeping process. Rather, place it gently in the cup with the string (if there is one) draped over the side, add water from the teapot, and leave it alone for about three minutes. And here's another no-no: When your tea has steeped, do *not* wind the string around the bag and spoon to squeeze out the excess. Instead, gently press the bag against the inside of your cup with your spoon to extract as much liquid as you can, then place the soggy thing in your saucer.

A note to prospective hostesses: please, please don't use teabags at parties. But if you must, put a number of them in a pot and let them steep rather than doling them out individually.

As with any hot beverage, you want to wait until your tea has cooled to a drinkable temperature before tasting it. Never blow on it or swish it around to cool it down. And when you are ready to sip, sit up straight and raise your teacup to your mouth; never bend to meet it.

Here's a point of etiquette you may not have been aware of. It is considered good manners to look into your cup while drinking, not over it. Take small sips, *never gulp*, and put your cup back down on the saucer between sips. And (do I need to tell you this?) *never* dip cookies or any other edible morsel into your tea.

Etiquette is grace, so never clink your teaspoon against the sides or rim of the cup as you stir. Rather, delicately fold your sweetener and milk into the tea by moving the spoon from the six o'clock position up to the twelve three times before placing it on your saucer. Place the spoon behind your teacup with the handle pointing right—or left if you're left-handed. If you prefer lemon to milk, add the sugar first, because the acid from the citrus will prevent it from dissolving. Once your condiments have been added and blended, don't use your spoon again until it's time for a refill.

Moving on to the lovely edibles, remember never to eat directly from the tiered tea service or—*horrors*—put back half-eaten food. Instead, put one or two treats on your own plate before tasting.

The protocol for sampling from the three-tiered service tray is described in detail in the previous chapter, but just as a reminder, always begin with the bottom tier—the scones and other baked goods—and work your way up to the savories and finally the sweets.

Above all, relax and enjoy yourself. The tradition of afternoon tea has endured because it is simply the nicest way to spend time with friends and loved ones. And don't be shy about asking for a takeaway box for any lovely tidbits you couldn't finish. All the best venues have special containers for the purpose—but I'd avoid calling it a "doggie bag."

CHAPTER 4

THE PERFECT POT OF TEA

N o tea party can be deemed a success unless the tea itself is top-notch. We all know the basics, but there might be a few details here you weren't aware of.

As in any recipe, a good result begins with good ingredients. Choose the highest-quality loose tea you can find, and allot one teaspoon per guest, plus one "for the pot." If using a perforated tea ball, make sure not to overfill it; you must leave enough room for the water to flow freely around and through. If making a large pot, several tea balls should be used.

Before adding the tea to the pot, scald the vessel by rinsing the inside with extremely hot water and swishing it around before emptying it out. This will help maintain the tea's temperature once it is made and ensure that once the first round is poured, the rest doesn't cool too rapidly. Tea purists insist that warming the cups in the same way is beneficial to the taste, so you might want to give each of them a scalding swirl at the same time.

Optimum water quality and temperature are also factors in making the perfect "cuppa." If possible, use fresh or bottled spring water, as it contains more oxygen than tap, and that can help bring out the tea's authentic flavor. And never reboil water that has been sitting in the kettle; this can introduce a metallic taste.

Water designated for black tea, alone, should be brought to a full boil at a temperature of approximately 200 degrees F and then poured directly over the tea leaves to bring out their rich flavor and aroma. Water for oolong tea should be heated to just below the boiling point (180-190 degrees F), while white and green

teas should be made with steaming water, heated to approximately 170 degrees F. For these delicate leaves, you might want to let your water cool in the kettle for a second or two before adding it to the teapot, as an extra safeguard again burning. Keep in mind that the longer water boils, the less oxygen it has, so ignore that adage about a "watched pot" and keep a careful eye on it.

Black and white teas should be left to steep the longest but never more than five minutes. Oolong is best at three-to-four minutes, and green is lovely in as little as thirty seconds but can be left for up to two minutes. Whatever the variety, just prior to serving, give the leaves a stir to balance the strength and oils, then discard them to prevent the release of bitter tannins.

As discussed earlier, tea should be served and passed one cup at a time as it tends to cool quickly. Once all of your guests have been served, fit a tea cozy over the pot to keep the remaining tea warm.

Unless you are adhering to the formal rules of service, the add-ons may be passed around—sugar first, followed by milk and lemon—so that your guests can take what they like.

What I've described here is ideal, but don't overthink your tea preparation—it is an art, not a science, and the process is meant to be enjoyed as much as the product. No need to discard what you've made and start over if you take your eye off the timer for a minute or two.

Heavy Metal

If possible, provide your guests with pearl spoons with which to stir their tea (and use one for that final swirl in the pot, too). These preserve the liquid's true, clear taste, while silver or stainless steel can tarnish it. If such items aren't available, a quick but elegant stir should be employed.

CHAPTER 5

UP FOR DEBATE

Milk Before or After?

During the 1800s, tea was served in soft-paste porcelain, which could crack or stain when hit with boiling water. The solution was to add a bit of milk to the cup to temper it, then pour the tea over the milk. (This was also believed to kill any harmful bacteria in milk that was a bit beyond fresh.)

With the advent of high-quality bone china, such as that created by Josiah Spode, shattering ceased to be a concern. People of means (and social climbers who wanted to appear like them) began pouring their tea into the cup first as an indication of the quality of both their china and the accompanying milk. If you've ever heard the phrase, "She's a milk-in-first sort of person," you now understand the slight.

There is one advantage to the milk-first preparation of tea. Even the most fastidious hostess can't prevent a few stray leaves from escaping their basket and ending up in the tea. When milk is added to the cup first, it tends to pull those errant leaves right to the bottom of the cup where they can't be seen. The explanation of this phenomenon rests in the milk's fat content. In addition, some note that the hasty addition of cold milk to hot tea breaks down the dairy proteins, changes the tea's flavor, and can cause a coat of skin to float on the top.

Today, nobody will make assumptions about your socio-economic status based on the order in which you assemble your tea, so feel free to do what feels right to you while considering these non-debatable facts: adding milk before tea permits its temperature to rise more slowly, making for a somewhat more decadent tea, while adding it after the tea can cause it to scald, making the concoction a little bitter.

As recently as the 1940s, it was possible to tell from where people hailed by the way they prepared their tea. In general, the British tended to begin with milk while the Europeans were tea-first all the way. The fashion has changed, however, and today the English—including Queen Elizabeth II, from what I have heard—have joined their European counterparts in starting with tea and then adding milk, though never cream. People the world over agree that cream belongs in coffee.

Pinkies Up or Down?

Now that our tea is ready to sip, let's discuss the pinkie thing. While poising your pinkie in the air seems a bit precious today, there was a reason to do so once. Because the earliest porcelain teacups, fabricated and used in China, were made without handles, a raised pinkie was helpful for balance. Handles were added in the 1700s, but they were still too delicate to get one's finger through, so the practice persisted.

By the 1800s, when afternoon tea was celebrated as a royal and upper-class pastime, the need to raise the pinkie was diminished, but the effect of it persisted; it just looked posh, whether hoisting a teacup or tea sandwich. (Of course, that sandwich was to be grasped with just three fingers—leaving the pinkie free to follow its own choreography.)

Fast forward to the 1961 film *Breakfast at Tiffany's,* where Audrey Hepburn could be seen taking tea with her baby finger fully erect. It had become not a sign of high social status but of the aspiration to become part of high society..

Scones

What's to debate about a scone, you might wonder? A variety of things, it turns out, starting with how the ideal scone should be made. The English take a more basic approach than their American counterparts. They don't use a lot of butter in their recipe and compensate for it by slathering the finished product with clotted or heavy whipped cream. They hold back on the sugar as well to allow for the addition of jam or preserves. In short, the British scone serves as a kind of canvas for fresh toppings provided at the table.

Americans (admittedly an excessive lot) use up to three times as much butter and double the sugar as the Brits while still not skimping on the toppers. Gilding the lily further, they often add such things as raisins or chocolate chips to the batter—pretty much unheard of in British scones. (Having already betrayed my weakness for sweets, it won't surprise you that I prefer the richer and sweeter American version—and am always delighted to see a few chocolate bits.)

Please Pass the . . . What?

Scones may be indisputably delicious, but how is their name pronounced? Does the word *scone* rhyme with *bone* or *gone*? There isn't a right or wrong answer to this one; again, it seems to be a matter of class. Those from posh, upper-crusty backgrounds—or those who wish they were—tend to use the latter pronunciation, while more down-to-earth types—including most Americans—prefer the former.

Saucer Sensibilities

What is there to say about the lowly saucer, beyond the fact that it goes under the cup to catch the drips? A few things.

From the 1700s well into the 1900s, the saucer was integral to the tea-drinking process. It was considered perfectly mannerly—even by the prim and fussy Victorians—to pour a small amount of the beverage from the cup into the saucer, then sip from the plate. From a practical standpoint, this made perfect sense, as the saucer's broad surface area sped up the cooling process so the tea could be consumed almost immediately rather than waiting for it to cool. When tea came into fashion in America, the practice was quickly adopted.

It seems that everything connected to the consumption of tea in England has a class element, and this practice is no different. An upper-class wife might

take pains to portray her leisurely station in life by allowing all the time in the world to let her tea cool in the cup while she gossiped with her friends. Busy working-class housewives and laborers didn't have that kind of time to waste and tended to pour their tea into the saucer for rapid cooling—especially those on a brief break from factory work. Space at the edge of the saucer might be reserved for some bread or a biscuit which, if a bit stale, would be allowed to soak up some of the tea to make it more palatable.

In the new world, the saucer-sipping custom even made it into an exchange between George Washington and Thomas Jefferson. Jefferson had been in France during the Constitutional Congress and had questions for Washington about why the delegates had decided to create two houses of Congress.

"Why did you pour that tea into your saucer?" Washington responded.

"To cool it," said Jefferson.

"Even so," said Washington, "we pour legislation into the senatorial saucer to cool it."

The practice remained common in America until the first half of the twentieth century, when it began to wane in most corners of society. Certainly, no one of the Baby Boomer generation or younger seems to indulge in it today—at least not in public. It's probably for the best, since saucer-sipping certainly raises the likelihood of drips onto tablecloths and clothing, and tea stains can be notoriously difficult to remove.

A quick aside regarding tea stains. Of course, first check the washing label of your garment to establish that it isn't "dry clean only." If it is washable, it's best to soak it in detergent as soon as possible so the stain doesn't set in. If that's not possible, and the stain is stubborn, try mixing one teaspoon of vinegar into a cup or so of water and spraying the mixture on the stain. Then gently blot your garment, and the stain should gradually lift. If it is still visible, rewet the stain and *gently* rub a teaspoon of baking soda into it. Let it sit for twenty minutes or so and rinse.

Cream or Jam first

Few topics within the world of tea are more contentious than the question of whether to apply cream or jam first to the surface of a warm scone. You'd think it would be a simple matter of taste, but outspoken discussion of the topic has persisted since the eleventh century.

The Cornish tradition is to spread the jam first, followed by clotted cream, while in Devon, the preference is to begin with the cream, then top it with local preserves. Team Devonshire explains that cream is similar to butter, and one would never consider trying to slather butter over jam. Cream on jam, they insist, just slides right off.

The Cornish maintain that it's easier to spread jam on bread, and that the richness of the cream can be better appreciated when it's on top. Their analogy is to fruit salad; one would never put cream *under* the fruit, would one?

Believe it or not, there are statistics on this. When last someone decided to take a poll, fifty-four percent of those questioned declared themselves "jam-firsters,"

while forty-six percent insisted that cream-before-jam is the only way to go. Pretty close. Maybe we should call it a draw, prepare our scones as we please, and move on to more pressing concerns. Or—even better—come up with a compromise.

That is exactly what the proprietors of New York City's Alice's Tea Cup did. Hailey and Lauren Fox, owners of the beloved chain of hip tea parlors, serve a *combination* of cream and jam. In that way, each "shmear" across one of their heavenly pumpkin scones provides the full jam/cream (or is it cream/jam?) experience.

Loose Leaf vs. Teabags

Having already made my preference quite clear, I want to end this chapter with a few more words about the glory of loose tea over teabags.

The world spins quickly these days, and we all need to find ways to relax. For me, tea is an integral part of the unwinding process. Beyond that, medical professionals agree that tea carries actual health benefits; it can contribute toward protecting us against heart disease and certain cancers.

Fine, I'll drink tea, you say—*but do I really have to go to the trouble of using the loose stuff?*

I admit that using loose tea requires a smidge more effort, but the benefits far outweigh the minor inconvenience. Loose tea produces a clearer and more flavorful drink, and when you take the extra few minutes to try it, I suspect you'll never go back.

As I explained earlier, teabags don't contain whole leaves but rather what is referred to as "dust" and "fannings." The meaning of *dust* is obvious, but what are *fannings*? Quite simply (and unpalatably), they are small pieces of tea leaves that have been rejected for use in premium grades of tea. Is it any wonder that teabags tend to create a duller, cloudier liquid with a flatter, less vibrant taste?

All I can do is urge you to forgo the bagged variety for a week in favor of some lovely loose-leaf and decide at that point how you want to take your tea. My guess is you won't go back to bags.

CHAPTER 6

LET'S MEET FOR TEA

A Few Unique and Lovely Rooms

There are literally thousands of fabulous tearooms worldwide—so many that it would take a giant volume (and all my teatimes for a decade) to mention them all. So, I'll confine myself to telling you about just a few of my favorites . . . and hope you are inspired to discover a few more of your own.

As I mentioned at the start, my lifelong pursuit of all things wonderful started the day my mother took me for tea at The Plaza Hotel—so where else to start our genteel journey?

The Plaza Hotel

768 FIFTH AVENUE
NEW YORK, NEW YORK

Designed by Henry Janeway Hardenberge in 1905, the magnificent Plaza Hotel was unveiled in all its opulence on October 1, 1907. (Construction took only twenty-seven months from start to finish—a whirlwind by today's standards.) Sparing no expense whatsoever, Hardenberg set out to invoke nothing less than a luxurious French chateau. The interior featured more than 1,650 chandeliers, imported Italian mosaic flooring, and specially designed doorknobs sporting the back-to-back P's that are still the hotel's monogram. The dining room offered its lavish fare on gold-rimmed china.

From the start, tea was served. At first it was proffered on the outdoor, canopied veranda known as the Champagne Porch. Later, the service was relocated to The Palm Court, the iconic hotel's central dining area, where it is still served today.

For over a century now, society mavens and the city's most discerning visitors have whiled away their afternoons over tea at The Palm Court, a stunning colonnaded room that comes into view immediately upon ascending the red-carpeted entry stairs to the lobby. Actual palm trees encircle the venue, lit softly by the sun filtering through its stained-glass domed ceiling. From the moment the host greets you and introduces you to your server, the personal touch prevails, and the pervasive feeling is one of genuine welcome. If you are concerned that such a grand place might seem intimidating, I urge you to visit and relish the lovely sense of belonging you will undoubtedly experience.

Over the decades the menu at afternoon tea has changed little—but if the offerings confuse you, your server will be happy to decipher the menu and make suggestions. Our etiquette maven, Myka Meiers, says of the Court's staff, "They are happy to help you satisfy your tastes perfectly in minutes. Just mention a food you enjoy, a taste you love, or even a mood you're in, and *snap,* they offer a wealth of knowledge, recommending specific teas and explaining why. There is simply nothing quite like afternoon tea at The Plaza."

When hosting clients, Meiers has been known to sit through three rounds of tea, back-to-back, on the same day—and of course the servers never let on. They simply reset the table and charmingly ask Ms. Meiers if she'll have "the usual" (which happens to be Tropical Garden infused tea accompanying an assortment of treats known as the "New Yorker"). If she's fortunate, she tells me, the chef might sneak her an extra of her favorite sandwich, the Scottish smoked salmon with paprika crème fraiche on pumpernickel.

The New Yorker is one of two never-changing classic offerings; the other is my own favorite, the Champagne Tea. Both selections include succulent and savory tea sandwiches such as tasty thyme-roasted prime rib with caramelized onions and horseradish, the ever-popular truffled chicken salad with black truffle aioli, and the aforementioned smoked salmon.

For an extra special splurge, or to celebrate a significant occasion, I recommend the Imperial Tea in all its grandeur. How can you not love a repast that begins with Petrossian Tsar Imperial Ossetra caviar washed down with Dom Perignon Champagne? Every morsel that follows is to be savored, from beet-and-goat-cheese gateaux, pocket-size lobster rolls, and supremely palatable duck liver pate to dulcet fresh-baked scones with Meyer lemon curd and house-made jams. This particular tea service is a bit pricey, but indisputably magical. You're bound to float home on a cloud.

Executive Pastry Chef Matthew Lambie has told me that he bakes the Court's sweet treats personally, including calamansi lime s'mores, maple and pecan cheesecake with a toasted pecan and graham cracker base, and the excellent Plaza chocolate-and-passion-fruit cake. These sweet treats may look a bit more petite than some others,

but Chef Matthew makes up for it by insuring there are a few extras on each top-tier tray.

Mindful of current dietary preferences, The Palm Court also offers a gluten-free tea service featuring such items as house-roasted turkey finished with cranberry aioli and brie and napoleon smoked salmon with pickled onion cream cheese. The sweets are surprisingly tasty, too. I highly recommend the green apple bavaroise and cranberry jelly pistachio cake.

The vegan tea menu features temptations too numerous to enjoy in a single visit—so come and try them all over several afternoons!

When my mother introduced me to tea at The Plaza they didn't offer a children's tea, but they do now. The Children's Afternoon Eloise Tea—named, of course, for that fictitious little hell-raiser dreamed up by Kay Thompson and Hilary Knight—is a rite of passage for many lucky little girls and boys. In this case, salmon and caviar make way for organic peanut-butter-and-jelly sandwiches on wheat bread and Parisian ham and gruyere cheese with pear grain mustard butter on a pretzel ficelle. Of course, the presentation wouldn't be complete without a selection of *rawther delicious* child-friendly beverages, including tropical strawberry basil garden, chamomile ginger ale, lemongrass verbena rooibos, and even a virgin mint julep. I've also seen pink peppermint candy cane cotton candy on a salty pretzel stick go by, and while I'm not sure how I feel about trying one, I've seen a few adults request one to go.

Part of the fun of tea at The Plaza is that you never know who you might see at a nearby table. I was once enjoying tea with the Oscar-winning actress Celeste Holm and her husband when we spied Aretha Franklin and her entourage. The view from afar was exciting enough, but my heart actually fluttered as Ms. Franklin crossed the room to pay her R-E-S-P-E-C-Ts to Celeste.

Myka Meier told me a story about a time when she was sitting with a client over tea, discussing business, when the man at the next table got up and prepared to leave. "He was immaculately dressed from head to toe and had been sitting by himself reading," Myka explained. "As he collected his belongings from the banquette, he made eye contact with my client, who said, 'Ha, for a second there, I thought you looked exactly like Tommy Hilfiger.' The man just smiled. I didn't tell my client that he was, in fact, Tommy Hilfiger, who happened to own a magnificent apartment on the residence side of the hotel. Of course, Tommy gave me a little conspiratorial wink before he departed—which was the best part."

In short, The Plaza and its Palm Court are timeless. It doesn't take an extravagant imagination to envision Zelda and F. Scott Fitzgerald sipping champagne in a corner, partially obscured by the ever lush and verdant palms.

The Fairmont Empress Hotel
7210 GOVERNMENT STREET
VICTORIA, BRITISH COLUMBIA
CANADA

Indulging in afternoon tea at the winsome Lobby Lounge of the Fairmont Empress Hotel in Victoria is another enchanting "under the palms" experience. The hotel's stunning stained-glass dome resembles that of New York's Plaza, though they have moved their tea service from under it to a location called the Tea Lobby. I suggest making reservations, as more than 400 guests experience the magical ritual daily and have been doing so since February 20, 1908.

Unlike some other afternoon teas, the Empress rendition is a designated stop for visiting British royals. After one such visit, in 1939, when King George VI and Queen Elizabeth hosted a dinner for 250 in the Empress Dining Room, they commissioned and shipped special china from a factory in Stoke-on-Trent, England, as a gift of appreciation to the hotel. As it is in many families, that priceless tableware was carefully packed away for use only on special occasions. (And when I say priceless, I don't just mean the china's historical significance. The pattern on that china was created by layering fourteen lithographic transparencies one over another, then hand-painting the result with twenty-two-carat gold.) It would be twelve years before it came out again for a royal visit from Princess Elizabeth.

Tea at the Fairmount Empress is well worth the excursion, if only to savor its unique tea blend—named the Empress Blend, of course—accompanied by

its world-famous Empress Cake. Blended by the Metropolitan Tea Company, the tea incorporates leaves from Ceylon, Assam, and India, resulting in a rich, full-bodied drink that is arguably one of the finest in the world. Experts have told me they enjoy inhaling the fragrant floral and fruity tones while taking small sips to prolong the experience.

Lest you think all this finery renders the place too posh for you, think again. The Empress welcomes children five and over and has a designated child-friendly service for cultivating your tykes' manners and taste for the finer things right from the beginning. After sampling organic peanut-butter-and-jelly and honey ham-and-cheese tea sandwiches, followed by homemade chocolate chip cookies, teddy bear macaroons, and vanilla lollipops, they won't even mind sitting at a table with the grown-ups. While the youngsters are enjoying these delicacies, the adults are treated to cinnamon-spiced squash-and-gruyere quiche, cold smoked pacific sockeye salmon, and poached Vancouver Island egg salad. Delectable sweets cap off the tea for everyone—and you might want to add a slice or two of that Empress Cake for the table to share.

About *that cake:* rest assured; it is no ordinary sweet. Executive Pastry Chef AJ Thalakkat developed the custom offering in France, and its dark chocolate is made from a combination of cocoa beans from Madagascar and Haiti. The chef blends this with milk chocolate infused with ingredients local to the Pacific Northwest, starting with honey from the hotel's beehives, hazelnuts from Oregon, and native blackcurrants. He finishes it off with homemade cassis, a dusting of cocoa powder, and a sprinkling of (gasp) edible gold dust.

This is not a venue at which to calorie count. If you're concerned, you might try to burn some off with an afternoon walk around the sparkling Victoria Inner Harbor or a stroll around the Vancouver Island District for shopping and sightseeing—and don't forget Butchart Gardens. They are fabulous.

In response to recent concerns over the dreaded Coronavirus, the Empress has started offering afternoon tea to go, featuring its signature delectables packed in a special three-section takeaway box to enjoy at a park, beside the water, or perhaps at the summit of Mount Doug.

The Lobby

THE PENINSULA HONG KONG
SALISBURY ROAD
TSIM SHA TSUI
KOWLOON, HONG KONG
CHINA

The Peninsula—once referred to as "the finest hotel east of the Suez"— is one of the oldest hotels in Hong Kong, having first opened its doors in 1928. I'm going to cut to the chase and urge you to book a visit to this amazing place if you possibly can. It is the epitome of grace and classic British colonial elegance and features—yes—*lush palm trees.* At the same time, it feels sleek and modern and offers state-of-the-art amenities. Is it any wonder that it's a magnet for celebrities and dignitaries from far and wide?

Just as at The Plaza, you never know who might sit down to tea at the table next to you. Past visitors include Princess Margaret, the Maharajah of Jaipur, and the Begum Aga Khan, as well as American Presidents Ronald Reagan and

Richard Nixon and film stars Warren Beatty, Charlie Chaplin, Shirley MacLaine, Marlon Brando, Clark Gable, Elizabeth Taylor, and many others.

The hotel is happy to send someone to pick you up at the airport in a luxurious Rolls Royce Phantom, or you might opt instead for a helicopter straight to the hotel's own rooftop helipad.

An important thing to note (and perhaps an enticement for a resident visit) is that only hotel guests can reserve a table for tea. Others must take their chances and queue up with hotel guests given priority. I've heard from numerous people that even if you arrive a few minutes prior to its two o'clock opening, you might well experience a two-hour wait—no chairs provided.

Once you've been granted your table, be prepared to settle in and fully savor your experience. Afternoon tea at the Peninsula is an old-world, decadent affair. The dramatic space features sky-high classical columns, stained-glass windows, gold-leaf-gilded plaster and wood accents, opulent gold and cream-colored seating, sparkling chandeliers, and gargoyles—yes, gargoyles. Gentle music provided by a string quartet floats down from a second-floor balcony.

The knowledgeable servers are impeccable in white suits, shirts or blouses, and bow ties. They move about discreetly while attending to every fallen crumb. With the assistance of a tea master, I opted for the Peninsula Classic afternoon tea selection and sipped a flute of champagne as I waited for it to arrive. As I sat, unwinding, I took in the lovely table settings, featuring crystal, flowers, and fine china, relishing the illusion that I was worth every bit of the quiet opulence surrounding me.

Soon, a heavy sterling-silver teapot arrived, and my chai tea was expertly filtered over a silver strainer, which was then laid to rest in another tiny silver receptacle. An additional silver pot of hot water was thoughtfully left so that I might enjoy a second cup without waiting.

As amazing as the tea service was, I didn't become truly giddy until the sweets and savories arrived on tiered silver platters. The food included everything I yearned for without knowing I'd been yearning: sweet bites, including the hotel's famous egg tart, on the top tier; savory canapes and finger sandwiches in the center; and perfect warm, raisin-riddled scones on the bottom. To say this was a traditional presentation should not in any way imply it was ho-hum. Far from it, the crustless sandwiches and savory tarts were perfectly seasoned and delicious, and the care and imagination that went into the sugary little bites, some in the form of flowers and others with gold dust sprinkled on them, made me almost reluctant to eat them. *Almost.* They tasted even better than they looked.

Through the years, the Peninsula's dress code has relaxed (for better or worse) to the point where the only staunch taboo is flip-flops. But I strongly suggest that you dress up because—if not at the Peninsula, then where? Go ahead and put on the dog. It's fun, and who knows? Perhaps the people at the next table will mistake you for one of the film stars who frequent the place.

Alice's Tea Cup

> *"Our concept was to take something traditional and turn it upside down—an edgy Alice who fell down that rabbit hole into New York City."*
> —Lauren Fox, co-proprietor of Alice's Tea Cup

Growing up on New York's Upper West Side, Lauren and Hailey Fox were influenced by their father, who, as Lauren puts it, "was the biggest tea drinker in the world. He had a huge, extra-tall glass mug that was never empty of his favorite Twining's English Breakfast Tea." As they tell it, their parents would bring home tea in tins from wherever they traveled until their apartment was filled with them. And in New York, the family would routinely go out for afternoon tea.

"From a young age, we knew what afternoon tea was and looked forward to each visit," recalled Hailey. "A hands-down favorite was The Palm Court followed by The Pierre and Rumpelmayer's."

The girls were raised on loose tea and learned the differences among the varieties to the point where they became little experts. "We were rather snooty about it, without meaning to be," said Lauren, "or even knowing we were. We just relished tea and the comraderie and pageantry of it all."

Eventually, Lauren and Hailey migrated to Los Angeles to work in the entertainment business, Lauren as an actress and Hailey in film development. But they never let go of the dream that *someday*—perhaps after they retired—they might open a tea shop of their own, similar to the one in L.A. they had begun to frequent. They knew they wanted to create something free-standing and not too "pinky-up," as they put it—a whimsical place of escape where there was no need to dress up, and where people would feel genuinely fed.

"Many times, we'd go for afternoon tea, and when we left, we felt like going somewhere else for a meal," Lauren explained. "We wanted to create a tea salon that wasn't just for dainty women and girls but that would appeal to men, too—really, all adults with a sense of the urban. We hoped it would have a bit of sexiness, and that's where our Alice-in-the-city concept came from."

Fast forward to September 2001. The sisters had landed back in New York, and on a neighborhood walk with her then-husband, Hailey spied a small shop with a "For Rent" sign. It seemed like the perfect spot for that tea salon they'd dreamt about. "Lauren was just back," Hailey explained, "and I called her and said, 'What do you think? Should we really do this before we retire?'"

Keep in mind that at this point, the two were still in their twenties, full of the exuberance of youth and nowhere near retiring. They signed the lease on September 12 and got to work immediately. Even with the tragedy that had just shattered the city—and made them question the importance of afternoon tea in a world turned upside down—they pushed forward. And their first shop, later designated Chapter I, was a success. It didn't hurt that Florence Fabricant from the *New York Times* wrote a glowing story that ran on the front page of the Metro section the day they opened their doors.

To staff the place, Lauren primarily hired friends with whom she thought it would be fun to work regardless of their knowledge of tea. "The idea was to create a kind of mad tea party," she told me. "We were intending a 'soft opening' to work the bugs out and train the staff. We didn't expect to be deluged by customers, but thanks to the *Times* article, there was a line down the block."

Twenty years and several "chapters" later, the sisters' original philosophy remains. All genders and ages are made to feel welcome, and although Alice's is not a children place, the vibe is decidedly childlike in some ways. The good food, as well as the top-notch tea selections and festive ambiance, have made it a favorite of celebrities, tourists, and locals alike. Katie Holmes and her daughter, Suri, have been photographed coming and going, as has Madonna—dragged there by her son who had visited with his babysitter and loved the crepes. Paul McCartney was once overheard on the street asking for directions to the shop.

Lauren and Hailey remain hands-on owners, unfazed by the starry attention. Lauren told me about a day at Chapter III when they were preparing for their annual health department inspection. "I was doing a final comb-through to make sure that the kitchen was sparkling," she said, "and I looked under the oven and could see way, way in the back a bit of grease. No one else would ever notice, but I was on a mission." She was running the front of the house that day and dressed for the purpose, so she asked one of the staff to clean it up and was informed that it was unreachable. "So, I rigged a broom end with gaffer tape," she said, laughing at her own obsessiveness, "put a towel around it, got down on my knees, and shimmied under the oven to wipe it down. I distinctly remember thinking, 'We have Suri Cruise hanging out in the restaurant having afternoon tea, and I'm in the kitchen covered in fryer grease. So glamorous!'"

Each location of Alice's Tea Cup is as full of personality as its proprietors. The staff is friendly, well-informed, and prepared to offer suggestions, and—even more important—the food is terrific. Some favorites—and not just mine—are the pumpkin scones and the curried chicken sandwiches. Just thinking about them makes my mouth water.

If you've never been, you must try one of the shops, and please let me know what your favorite food and tea selections were. I'm betting on the Mad Hatter Tea! Of course, if you're a regular, I'd love to hear from you, too.

Restaurant Le Dalí
LE MEURICE
DORCHESTER COLLECTION
228 RUE DE RIVOLI
PARIS, FRANCE

Each venue I introduce you to is a distinctive oasis—which is why I could never omit this unique and unforgettably "artsy" venue in the heart of Paris.

I'll describe it by sharing my personal experience there. From the moment the host, Jennifer, escorted me to my sofa—featuring cushions festooned with Salvador Dalí images—I knew I was in for a treat. And believe it or not, I was impressed by what was served next: water. The thing is, it wasn't just tap water or even the bottled stuff, but a cool blend of water, mint, and lemon—and the effect of sipping it was instant relaxation. I sat back to savor it and admire my surroundings—including the amazing Ara Starck ceiling, which I'll come back to later—before even glancing at the menu.

The offerings were simple: A choice of Dalí's Tea Time, Champagne Tea Time, or Cocooning Tea Time. The first included a presentation of finger sandwiches, homemade scones with jams and cream from nearby Paris Borniambuc farm, pastry chef Cedric Grolet's selections of the day, and tea, coffee, or Alain Ducasse hot chocolate. The second included all of the above plus Veuve Clicquot Ponsardin Champagne. And the Cocooning Tea Time was all that plus a facial and massage! Now . . . I rarely turn down a body treatment, but somehow this "add-on" seemed out of keeping with the tea experience, so I opted for the champagne. (I know . . . big surprise.)

Here's where Le Dalí separates itself from other tea salons. Cedric Grolet actually creates sweets using Dalí's iconic imagery. On one of my visits, my server, Hugo, ceremoniously presented the three-tiered tray and explained precisely how I was to proceed. Like much else about this place, it wasn't traditional. He instructed me to begin with the top tier, on which were nestled three creations that looked as if they belonged in the Dalí Museum. One looked like a peach with a white chocolate shell that, when broken, expelled the most fabulous blend of peach jam, cake, and diminutive peach bites. Another was a surrealistic cherry made of cake, real cherries, and cherry liqueur; and the last

was a beautiful chocolate cookie topped with raspberries. This was art at its most edible—or would you say food at its most artistic? Eventually, I descended to the sandwich selections, which included lobster, salmon, and ham, and finally to the scones. From that moment, I vowed to start all my tea services with the dessert tier, and I have Hugo to thank for it. I mean . . . life is short, right?

I'd be remiss if I didn't mention the tea itself. Lydia Gautier has traveled the world for over twenty years to find the rarest and most flavorful blends available, so I suggest you leave your comfort zone and try one you might never get another opportunity to enjoy. I had the Japanese green tea and enjoyed it thoroughly.

Now, back to that Ara Starck ceiling. Over the years, Ms. Starck's famous father—well-known Parisian artist and interior designer Phillipe Starck—was commissioned to renovate various aspects of the prestigious Le Meurice. When he decided to add a dramatic ceiling mural over the glass dome of the winter garden, Ara submitted her vision anonymously, and it was selected. It is truly spectacular: a gargantuan gold and ochre canvas depicting the most festive aspects of hotel nightlife and measuring more than 1,500 square feet. Jennifer told me that it had taken ten men more than sixteen hours to install the painting, which Ara had begun in her own workspace and completed in a studio for fabricating movie sets.

Do you understand now why I insist you visit this marvelous establishment? I'll only add that this paean to the art world has been visited not only by Dalí himself—who considered it his second home—but Picasso, Andy Warhol, and numerous other greats. I can easily imagine Salvador's famous mustache peeking over a flute of Veuve as he enjoyed his Champagne Tea Time.

Salon Proust

> *"When I dream of afterlife in heaven,*
> *the action always takes place in the Paris Ritz."*
> —Ernest Hemingway

It was as if the gods were conspiring to keep me from enjoying tea at Salon Proust in the iconic Ritz Hotel. In 2011, when I'd planned a visit there, the hotel closed for the first time in its lengthy history for a massive, four-year renovation. Then, just as it was about to reopen in 2016, a fire delayed the unveiling further. We all know what happened in 2020: Covid shuttered the Ritz just as it did every other public place. So, when I finally made it to the evocative hotel in 2021, it was a truly special experience.

The Ritz has long been synonymous with luxury and elegance, and in the old days, the place could be a bit intimidating. I suppose they had a right to their haughtiness. After all, Coco Chanel called it home for more than thirty years, and other residents included F. Scott Fitzgerald and Marcel Proust. Ernest Hemingway visited so often that they named a bar for him. Sophia Loren dubbed it "the most romantic hotel in the world," and Ingrid Bergman chimed in her plaudits, too. Who am I to disagree with people who could stay anywhere in the world they chose?

As I entered the Salon Proust, I felt as if I were visiting a dear friend for a catch-up over a soothing pot of tea à la Française. The room itself is a warm, wood-paneled library lined with shelves of first editions, plush armchairs, and a fireplace that crackles to life during the chillier months. My table was set with Limoges china adorned with a golden madeleine motif, a nod to the famous opening of Proust's *In Search of Lost Time*.

After a warm greeting, I was told that, while they had numerous tea services to choose from, the distinctive Gouter à la Française (taste of France) had been suggested for me. Apparently, the "French way" is to enjoy one's tea with sweets exclusively—no savories. Okay by me! All that was left was to choose a particular tea (or coffee) and decide whether I wanted champagne.

First things first: big yes to the champagne—which turned out to be a perfect glass of the Ritz Reserve Barons de Rothschild. Then came a Ritz signature tea tradition: an *amuse bouche* of a madeleine soaked in clove-infused milk, served in a teacup. It was surprisingly refreshing.

I could have floated home on a cloud right then, but I'd have missed the sweetest of feasts. At exactly the right moment, the traditional three-tiered cake stand arrived, laden with beautiful cigarettes russes, madeleines, cakes, and chocolate tarts, courtesy of pastry chef extraordinaire François Perret. I couldn't possibly have finished it all—as badly as I wanted to—but no worries; everything left on the trays when I pushed myself back from the table was packed carefully into a Hotel Ritz takeaway box for midnight snacking—along with a gift packet of house-blend tea to accompany the leftovers.

This was one of the nicest two-and-a-half hours I'd spent in a long while and well worth waiting out renovations and pandemics to spend it. For your sake and mine, I hope the place thrives for many decades to come.

The Tea House on Los Rios

31731 LOS RIOS STREET
SAN JUAN CAPISTRANO, CALIFORNIA

I want to tell you about this wonderful place, but before I do, I must say a few words about its surroundings in one of the oldest neighborhoods in California. Visiting the Los Rios Historic Downtown District in San Juan Capistrano is like stepping back in time and experiencing the high points of the myriad cultures—Native American, Mexican, European—that have made their mark on the area over its 240-plus-year history. These include Mission San Juan, founded by Junipero Serra (now a saint) on November 1, 1776—long before California was a state. You've probably heard about the swallows that migrate 6,000 miles from Argentina to land here each March 19, a miracle witnessed by visitors from around the globe as part of St. Joseph's Day.

The city has also preserved three of the original adobe houses occupied by mission and ranch families around the turn of the eighteenth century. Another

must-see is the 1894 train depot—still in operation—that now also houses a restaurant and an art gallery. It retains its original forty-foot-high dome, mission bell, arches, and other architectural details.

Once you've toured these historic sites, you'll be more than ready for tea. The Tea House on Los Rios is located in the midst of all this unique history, in a lovingly restored 1911 cottage ringed by an inviting wrap-around veranda. It's a serene and enchanting spot presided over by Damien, the third generation of his family to run the place. From the start, when his grandparents first opened the venue, the entire family has been involved. Damien is the oldest grandchild and told me he helped lay bricks when he was ten and progressed to busing tables and then waiting on them while he was in college working toward his accounting degree. Seven years later, after earning that degree and securing a job as a CPA, he realized that his job—although stable and lucrative—didn't "feed his soul" the way the tea house had, so he returned. His younger brothers Justin and Christopher are now working there too, while attending school just as their big brother did.

The Tea House offers five unforgettable tea service experiences, and I must say they are generously portioned. The Victorian Tea—the most generous of the lot—happens to be my personal favorite, though I have sampled several others when I'm not quite so ravenous. The Victorian includes your choice of a flute of champagne, a mimosa, or a glass of sparkling cider; soup and salad; exceptionally tasty finger sandwiches; scones with preserves and cream; fresh fruit; mouthwatering desserts; and a lively assortment of loose teas. The Mission Tea is similar but a bit less fulsome, with a choice of soup *or* salad; and the offerings proceed down the line through The Garden Tea, The Los Rios Tea, and The Cottage Tea, which simply features soup, scones, and fruit.

Lest you think young palates have been forgotten, there's The Treehouse Tea, a special for kids, featuring a choice of peanut-butter-and-jelly, grilled cheese, or turkey sandwiches along with a scone and fresh fruit. Child-friendly beverages include tea, pink lemonade, and a Shirley Temple.

In addition to afternoon tea, The Tea House on Los Rios offers a full lunch menu featuring a wonderful shepherd's pie, rosemary chicken, English pasti, and a Bombay chicken curry to die for. For those with daintier appetites, creative entrée salads include the Queen Mum's Spring Salad, another favorite of mine. Its weekend brunch wouldn't be complete without a perfectly concocted Bloody Mary or mimosa.

Whatever the time of day you visit or occasion you happen to be celebrating, The Tea House on Los Rios will remind you that you don't have to go to an international city to experience gracious hospitality steeped in history. You might even vow to return as often as the swallows do!

Sketch
9 CONDUIT STREET
LONDON, UNITED KINGDOM

In a city within a country that is renowned for its afternoon tea, Sketch is a quirky must-visit. I was initially intrigued by all the discussion of it that seemed to revolve around the restrooms. "You have to go to the bathroom there!" exclaimed everybody I queried about the place. *Um . . . okay,* I thought, and off I went, hoping the tea might be worthwhile, too.

I found the surrounding neighborhood of Mayfair nice but rather ordinary and was happy to see that the shop itself was in a historic building dating back to 1779. From a well-informed member of the staff, I learned that it had once been

the site of the Royal Institute of British Architects and the London atelier of the iconic haute couture house, Christian Dior.

Once I'd made it through the portals, the ordinary vanished, and I was mesmerized by the magic that surrounded me. If you go, I urge you to pay attention to every detail—starting with the hopscotch grid on the floor and swath of paint seemingly cascading down a stairway. Word of caution here: if, unlike me, you abhor the color pink, turn around and leave. From the walls to the cushions to the staff uniforms to the aforementioned toilets, the color is everywhere, thanks to designer India Mahdavi and fashion designer Richard Nicoll. Well-known illustrator and satirist David Shrigley is responsible for the lively drawings that adorn the walls and distinctive ceramic tableware. (Check the bottom of your cup for a witty surprise!)

Once my eyes had adjusted to the visual cacophony, I was directed to my table where the voluminous tea menu awaited. Again, my mind was boggled, and I had to settle into my plush cocoon and wait for the Tea Master (a kind of Tea Sommelier, really) to assist me. He soon materialized and walked me through the selections, even proffering samples of the leaves so that I might select based on scent. It was by far the most personal attention I have ever received as part of this process. In the end, he suggested that I pick two types of tea, one to accompany the savory nibbles and the other for the sweets—a brilliant idea to which I assented immediately.

In an afternoon of firsts, the initial course was yet something else new to me: an egg with a souffle consistency and cheese straws to dip into it. I assumed that's what they were for, but before I could take my first dip, someone I can only describe as the Caviar Man arrived to offer a generous dollop of the precious stuff and a fascinating tutorial on how to eat it. Nobody has to talk me into caviar, so I was thrilled.

Mind you, this was all before the official tea course, which arrived as soon as the starter was discreetly cleared. The three-tiered tray was groaning with goodies, starting with scones accompanied by the best-ever clotted cream and jam selection. Sandwiches included egg gougere, coronation chicken on malted brown bread, and salmon and ricotta on brown bread. (I'm told that an array of vegetarian sandwiches can be had as an alternative, including vegan chicken, cucumber, and asparagus on crustless white bread, and avocado and tomato.)

It is in the dessert department that the British tea establishment really shines, and Sketch is no exception. Victoria sponge cakes, blackberry marshmallows, salted caramel eclairs, and Mara des Bois Battenberg cake all passed my lips—and if I close my eyes, I can still summon up their perfection.

Sketch's tea service offerings include the standard variations with kind consideration of vegetarians and pescatarians—and of course there is a champagne option, which I did not refuse. But I want to mention one final thing that sets this place apart from all others I know: you may ask for seconds. Or thirds. When it comes to afternoon tea at Sketch, there is simply no limit.

And—oh, yes—about those vaunted bathrooms. Any description I might offer wouldn't do the colors, lights, and egg-pod toilets justice, so I suggest you consult Instagram for the full effect. Better yet—visit them yourself.

La Galerie des Gobelins

HÔTEL PLAZA ATHÉNÉE
25 AVENUE MONTAIGNE
PARIS, FRANCE

Right out of the gate, I must confess my bias. The Hôtel Plaza Athénée is my all-time favorite home away from home—and who can blame me? This Parisian icon—located in the city's "Golden Triangle" within the posh Eighth Arrondissement—is luxurious yet friendly right from the start, its exterior featuring climbing vines, red awnings, and window boxes filled with scarlet geraniums. The interior is the epitome of Parisian chic and understated opulence, with high ceilings graced by glittering chandeliers and suspended crystals that illuminate a cream and gold color scheme.

In 2012, the hotel was awarded France's official "Palace" distinction, which represents the highest honor an establishment may obtain. The place even has its own signature

fragrance, which must be one of the reasons that stepping inside makes me feel instantly light-hearted.

We'll talk about tea in a moment, but let's dwell for a bit longer on the location. From the Plaza's renowned avenue Montaigne address, you are treated to magnificent views of the Eiffel Tower. It is a perfect jumping-off point for a stroll up the Champs Elysée—perhaps the most famous street in the world—a meander along the Seine, or a window-shopping spree along the avenue of *haute couture*, begin-

ning with the House of Dior (est. 1947) right next to the hotel. Other designer ateliers you'll pass include those of Louis Vuitton, Chanel, Max Mara, and Prada.

As you might imagine for such a venue and location, the Plaza A. has been a favorite stop for celebrity guests from around the globe. Elizabeth Taylor, Richard Burton, and their entourage once stayed for six months (can you imagine the price tag?), and a couple other favorite guests of yore were Josephine Baker and Rudolph Valentino. I actually saw Catherine Deneuve—the French film star and legendary beauty—with my own eyes, sipping tea in the hotel's Gallerie des Gobelins.

Like The Plaza Hotel in New York, the Plaza Athénée has served as a location for many movies and television shows. Two of its onscreen appearances that I enjoyed most were in the final episode of *Sex in the City* and the grand finale of the film *Something's Gotta Give,* featuring Jack Nicholson and Diane Keaton.

Enough about the setting, let's get to the seating! Afternoon Tea in La Gallerie begins with the strains of live harp music, which add a heavenly note to even the most mundane occasion. The décor of the room is every bit as elegant and tasteful as that of the rest of the hotel, including more crystal chandeliers, the most gorgeous mosaic floor you're likely to encounter in a public establishment, and lavish Louis XVI low-style table seating, which is easier to sink into than arise from and extremely plush and comfortable while you are sitting.

When it comes to your repast, you'll notice some differences from other tea services. For one thing, scones are completely absent. You won't be disappointed long, however, as they are replaced by an array of French classics such as madeleines, Paris-Brest, Mont-Blanc cake (a nod to the UK), tuiles, and—a personal obsession—Merveille Cake, which is a lemon meringue miracle, indeed.

Finger sandwiches aren't a staple here either. Instead, along with the best sweet afternoon tea in Paris, you'll be offered your choice of something a bit heartier. The last time I visited, I opted for the McCarthy Salade Caesar du Beverly Hills accompanied by a glass of rosé champagne. (This was a dish I'd enjoyed at the Polo Lounge in Los Angeles on numerous occasions, and it seemed like fun to compare it to a version prepared by a French chef.) You might want to choose something a little more Parisian, such as a croque monsieur or madame, or a French club sandwich. Just bear in mind that if you do select a sandwich, it is considered gauche to pick it up. If you don't want to attract haughty stares, cut it with a fork and knife as you would a steak—and that's that.

It's easy to understand why chef Angelo Musa was awarded a coveted *Meilleur Ouvrier de France* (Best Craftsman of France) and the title of World Champion in the pastry category. Not that Monsieur Musa allowed himself time to rest on his laurels. On the contrary, he got back to work and scored yet another title—that of Best Pastry Chef of the Year at the Relais Desserts Excellence Prizes. Consider yourself among the world's most fortunate as you sit and sample his wares.

It seems I say this about every establishment I have chosen to write about—and I guess that's because I consider it important—but be sure to linger over your repast, soaking in not just the tastes and smells but every detail of your surroundings. Tea at this or any of my favorite locations represents the good life at its best. Enjoy!

CHAPTER 7

WHAT'S WHAT: DEFINITIONS

Surely, you've gathered by now that for me, tea is much more than a beverage; it's an art form. And like all art forms, it has a vocabulary and language all its own. What follows are some of the key terms you need to understand in order to navigate the delightful realm of tea.

AFTERNOON TEA/ LOW TEA/FULL TEA: Today, tea is primarily a social affair, but the ritual began as a means for the upper classes to bridge the time between breakfast and dinner (which was served beginning at eight o'clock). There was no formal lunch break. It is frequently referred to as *low tea* because it is traditionally served on sofas or low chairs.

CLOTTED TEA: This delectable drink goes by a variety of names and is often referred to as Devonshire or Cornish cream tea. It is made by heating or steaming whole cow's-milk cream, then slowly cooling it. The procedure brings yellowish "clots" to the surface that can be spread like butter on bread or, more commonly, scones.

CREAM TEA: This term generally refers to a simple repast of scones with cream and jam.

ELEVENSIES: There's a name for the "midmorning slump" we experience between eleven and twelve o'clock in the morning, and this is it. It is easily ameliorated by a nice cup of tea and a snack.

FINGER SANDWICHES: It's unclear whether these dainty morsels derive their name from their shape or from the means by which we eat them, but you get the idea. These crustless little sandwiches are an integral part of most tea services and feature savory fillings such as smoked salmon, chicken salad, or roast beef, garnished with watercress, cucumber, or simply butter.

HIGH TEA/ MEAT TEA: This term applies to an evening meal eaten at five o'clock or later. It is heartier than low tea, usually includes some form of meat, and was originally formulated to accommodate famished factory workers during the Industrial Revolution. The word *high* in this context refers not to class but to the chairs one generally sits in to enjoy it. (You won't find a lot of high tea served nowadays.)

LIGHT TEA: As you'd expect, this is a lighter version of afternoon tea that typically includes scones and pastries but not sandwiches.

MILK TEA: One is never too young to develop the tea habit, and this is a great starter for children, featuring a beverage made up of three-quarters milk to one-quarter tea.

PASTRIES: In British parlance (the *lingua franca* of tea), this refers to cookies, truffles, and shortbreads.

ROYALE TEA: When afternoon tea includes a spirit such as champagne, sherry, or gin, it is *royale,* indeed.

SAVORIES: To tea lovers, the entire world may be divided into two categories: sweet and savory, with *savory* referring to the delicacies found on the middle tier of the tea tray: finger sandwiches and such.

SCONES: These dense, crumbly shortcakes form the foundation of afternoon or cream tea and are generally found on the bottom tier of the tray.

TEA CAKES: These small, toasted yeast rolls or cakes aren't overly sweet. Flavored with dried fruit and savory spices such as nutmeg, cloves, and cinnamon, they are the perfect complement to the tea itself.

CHAPTER 8

INTERESTING TEABITS

Children's Tea Sets

Starting in the late 1800s, little girls began to enjoy pretend tea parties, complete with a miniature china tea set. But these dishes weren't originally meant to be toys. The mini services were actually created as samples for salesmen of fine china, who found it more practical to carry the much smaller pieces from house to house than to lug their full-size counterparts. Their customers—most of whom were mothers—insisted on purchasing the diminutive sets for their children, and tea parties for tots were born.

Teabags

The earliest patent for a teabag dates back to 1901, but it was in 1908 that William Sullivan inadvertently commercialized the innovation by sending tea leaf samples to his customers in hand-sewn silk bags rather than the more traditional tea tins. Misunderstanding his intention—that the leaves be removed from the bags before preparation—they dropped the bags directly into boiling water and a revolution began. Sullivan was soon inundated with orders for the convenient little bags. It would take until the mid-1930s to perfect the cheesecloth tea bag, which wouldn't really catch on in stuffy old England until the 1970s.

Tea Roses

In Europe during the mid-nineteenth century, imported tea was often perfumed with flowers to give it a pleasing aroma. During this same period, a new variety of beautiful, fragrant roses began appearing around the continent. Because they reminded people of the fragrant tea they'd come to enjoy, the flowers were dubbed *tea roses*.

Iced Tea

A recipe for iced tea first appeared in 1877 in a cookbook called *Housekeeping in Old Virginia* by Marion Cabell Tyree. But credit for popularizing what has become a summer staple must go to a tea dealer named Richard Blechynden. At the Saint Louis World's Fair in 1904, Blechynden endeavored to hand out cups of Indian tea in an attempt to grow the American audience for the brew. But the weather was swelteringly hot and humid, and few wanted anything to do with the hot drink. In an attempt to salvage his investment, he plopped a few ice cubes  into the cups and interest picked up. Presto—a taste sensation was born.

Statistics

More than 159 million Americans drink tea daily, consuming over 1.42 million pounds each and every day. Here are some other facts and figures.

- Black tea is sometimes referred to as red tea because of its reddish tint.
- More than 200 cups of tea can be made from just one pound of tea leaves.
- The Turkish population consumes the most tea of any country worldwide, with an average of seven pounds per person.
- The Irish finish second, averaging about five pounds per tea drinker.
- The only state in the U.S. that can boast of having a working tea plantation is South Carolina, where the American Classic brand is produced. It is, of course, the official White House tea.
- Worldwide, over three million *tons* of tea are produced annually.
- The ditty "I'm a Little Tea Pot Short and Stout" was written by Clarence Kelley and George Harry Sanders in 1939.
- Tea plants require at least 50 inches of rain annually to thrive.
- Herbal and spiced teas are not technically tea because they don't contain tea leaves.
- The Boston Tea Party of 1773 was initially referred to as the Destruction of the Tea because tea parties wouldn't be so named until the 1830s.

- Teabags were a part of a soldier's rations during World War I.
- Earl Grey tea was named after Charles Grey—an actual Earl who repeatedly praised the frequent diplomatic gifts he received of tea flavored with bergamot oil. Tea merchants soon began offering the specially flavored blend to the public under the brand name Earl Grey.
- Tasseography is the art of tea leaf reading.

CHAPTER 9

RECIPES

A few of the tea rooms profiled in these pages were kind enough to share some treasured recipes, as were several of my British friends upon whom I have relied in researching this book. Thank you, tea purveyors, as well as Carol, Denise, and Beverly for passing along your mothers' and grandmothers' secrets.

Let's start with two of the treats that have made Alice's Tea Cup a must-visit for celebrities and commoners alike. "One of our brilliant bakers thought to incorporate our highly popular banana bread with Nutella and our cream cheese frosting," explains co-proprietor Lauren Fox. "We even pipe Nutella on top of the cake!"

Banana Nutella Cake

Makes one 8-inch, three-layer cake

FOR THE CAKE:
3 cups all-purpose flour
1½ teaspoons baking soda
¼ teaspoon kosher salt
¾ cup (1½ sticks) unsalted butter, brought to room temperature
2 cups sugar
3 eggs
1½ cups buttermilk
1 teaspoon pure vanilla extract
2 very ripe bananas, mashed

FOR THE CREAM CHEESE FROSTING:
1 stick (½ cup) butter, brought to room temperature
1½ cups cream cheese, brought to room temperature
3 cups confectioners' sugar

FOR THE FILLING AND DECORATION:
2 cups Nutella (2 13-ounce jars)

1. Preheat the oven to 350 degrees F.

2. In a medium bowl, whisk the dry ingredients together.

3. In a large bowl, use a mixer to cream the butter and sugar until light and fluffy. One at a time, add the eggs and mix until well blended. With the mixer

set to low, add the dry mixture a little bit at a time, alternating with the buttermilk and vanilla, mixing just until smooth. Use a spatula to gently fold in the mashed bananas.

4. Pour the batter evenly into the three cake pans and bake for 20-25 minutes or until a toothpick inserted into the center of the cakes comes out clean. Set the layers aside to cool completely in the pans before frosting.

5. To make the frosting, use a mixer to cream the butter and cream cheese in a large bowl until it is entirely combined and smooth. With the mixer set on the lowest speed, slowly add the confectioners' sugar, mixing until it is completely incorporated and the frosting is fluffy.

6. Frost each layer with Nutella (you won't use it all) and stack. Spread the cream cheese frosting over the top and sides. Using a piping bag with a 12 mm or 14 mm tip, pipe five concentric circles of Nutella around the top of the cake, starting with one small one in the center and increasing the size of the circles as you work your way out. Run a butter knife from the center outward across the top of the frosting, alternating with scores in the opposite direction (outer circle to the center) until you have gone completely around the cake.

Pumpkin Scones

3 cups all-purpose flour

⅓ cup sugar

½ teaspoon baking soda

2½ teaspoons baking powder

¾ teaspoon kosher salt

2 tablespoons ground ginger (or less for a milder flavor)

2 tablespoons ground cinnamon (or less for a milder flavor)

¾ cup (1½ sticks) unsalted butter, cut into ½-inch pieces

1¼ cups buttermilk

1 cup canned pumpkin puree (all pumpkin, not pumpkin pie filling)

2 tablespoons pure vanilla extract

CARAMEL GLAZE

1 cup (2 sticks) unsalted butter

1 cup firmly packed light brown sugar

½ teaspoon freshly squeezed lemon juice

¼ teaspoon kosher salt

½ cup heavy cream

1. Preheat the oven to 425 degrees F.

2. In a large mixing bowl, combine the flour, sugar, baking soda, baking powder, salt, ginger, and cinnamon.

3. With clean hands, work the butter into the dry mixture until it is thoroughly incorporated, and the mixture is the consistency of fine breadcrumbs.

4. Make a well in the center of the dry ingredients and pour the buttermilk, pumpkin puree, and vanilla extract into the well. Using your hands, combine the ingredients gently until the dry mixture is thoroughly wet—but do not knead!

5. Turn the mixture onto a floured surface and gather it together. Gently pat the dough to form a disk about 1½ inches thick. Using a 3 or 3½-inch biscuit cutter, cut as many scones as you can and lay them on a nonstick baking sheet. Gather the remaining dough together—again, without kneading—so you can cut out more scones.

6. Bake the scones for about 12 minutes or until lightly browned. Let them cool on the baking sheet for about 20 minutes before glazing them.

7. While the scones are cooling, prepare the caramel glaze. Place the butter, brown sugar, lemon juice, and salt in a saucepan over medium heat and whisk gently until the mixture is smooth. Just as the mixture comes to a light boil, add the heavy cream and reduce the heat to low. Whisk well for two minutes or until the glaze is thickened and smooth, then remove the pan from the heat.

8. To glaze a scone, hold it by the bottom, dip the top in the warm caramel glaze, and place it back on the baking sheet.

Scotch Eggs

This next one was a particular favorite of my friend Carol's father. Scotch eggs are good hot but even better cold. They are a longstanding staple on tea tiers. This recipe makes six servings but can easily be scaled up or down; just figure 2 eggs and ¼ pound of sausage for each Scotch egg.

6 hardboiled eggs, shelled and set aside
1½ pounds cooked sausage
12 eggs
1 cup breadcrumbs
Oil for frying

1. Beat 6 uncooked eggs and season with salt and pepper to taste, then mix in the cooked sausage. Beat and season the remaining 6 eggs and set aside.

2. Flour the hardboiled eggs and wrap them with the cooked sausage mixture, making sure the eggs are completely covered.

3. Brush each sausage-covered egg with the beaten and seasoned egg mixture, then roll in breadcrumbs.

4. Fry the eggs in a pan with oil until the sausage coverings are firm and golden brown. Serve either hot or cold.

Curried Chicken Sandwiches

7 ½ ounces boneless chicken
2 teaspoons chunked mango
2 teaspoons butter
3 slices rye bread
½ medium onion, sliced
¼ teaspoon fresh basil, chopped
Oil to coat chicken
1 teaspoon curry powder
¼ teaspoon fresh sage, chopped

1. Preheat the oven to 425 degrees F.
2. Cut chicken into pieces and put into a bowl with onion, curry powder, and herbs. Mix with enough oil to coat.
3. Spread mixture on a baking pan and cook for 20 minutes, then cool.
4. Transfer chicken mixture and liquid from cooking into a food processor and chop to a chunky consistency.
5. Add mango and season to taste.
6. Butter both sides of bread slices.
7. Spread mixture on one piece of bread, then top with the second. Spread another layer of the mixture on top of that and top with the third piece of bread.

8. Carefully cut the crusts off the sandwiches, then cut them into interesting smaller shapes.

Smoked Salmon Sandwiches

3 to 5 thin slices smoked salmon
1 teaspoon mayonnaise
1 teaspoon cream cheese
1 teaspoon fresh dill, finely chopped
2 slices rye or white bread, crusts cut off

1. Cream together cream cheese and mayonnaise. Add dill and season with salt
    and pepper to taste.

2. Spread mixture onto each slice of rye bread.

3. Add salmon and roll each piece, then slice into rounds.

Jam Roly-Poly

My editor doesn't think this high-carb sweet is posh enough to be included, but I must disagree. Although it's never truly caught on in the United States, I've loved the confection since my mother read me Beatrix Potter's Tale of Samuel Whiskers *or* The Roly-Poly Pudding *and I begged her to make it for me. English puddings date back to before the seventeenth century but were originally savory. Eliza Acton changed that in 1845, with her recipe for a sweet pudding that included the addition of mincemeat, jam, or marmalade. Children delighted in requesting "Dead Man's Arm" or "Shirt-sleeve Pudding," thus named because the pudding was typically steamed and served in muslin from old shirts. Today, it is traditionally steamed, boiled, or baked and served with custard.*

1 sheet of store-bought pie pastry
1 jar unsweetened jam (blackberry, blueberry, strawberry—whatever your preference)

1. Preheat the oven to 400 degrees F.
2. Press pastry into a 9-inch oblong pan so that it covers the bottom.
3. Spread generously with the jam, leaving about ½ inch uncovered all around.
4. Carefully roll the pastry lengthwise and seal the ends by pinching them.
5. Bake for approximately 35 minutes or until golden brown.

Devonshire Scones

Because this is a Devonshire scone, it is customary to lead with the jam when garnishing it.

2 cups all-purpose flour
3 tablespoons butter
½ teaspoon baking soda
1 teaspoon cream of tartar
1 teaspoon sugar
Pinch of salt
¼ to ½ cup sour milk (also known as buttermilk)

1. Preheat the oven to 465 degrees F.
2. Cut the butter into the flour until you have a crumbly mixture, then add in the rest of the ingredients and just enough sour milk to form a soft dough.
3. Roll the dough to a thickness of about ½ inch, then, using an English muffin cutter or upside-down teacup, cut out rounds.
4. Bake for 5-10 minutes or until golden.
5. Serve with jam and clotted cream.

Queen Anne's Lemon Curd

The original method for making this treat was to add lemon to cream and then press it through a cheesecloth to separate the curds from the whey. Today's version makes a smoother, more luscious custard that is delicious on warm scones. It can also be spread on bread or toast or used as a pie, cake, or tart filling. Apparently, it was a favorite of the royal who shares its name.

10 egg yolks
4½ cups sugar
1½ cups lemon juice, plus 2 tablespoons (you should be able to gather the 2 tablespoons
    from half a lemon)
½ teaspoon salt
1 cup (2 sticks) of butter
Zest from 4 lemons
1 8-ounce packet unflavored gelatin
1 tablespoon cold water

1. Combine egg yolks, sugar, and lemon juice in a heavy pot and stir over medium heat until just boiling.

2. Add remaining ingredients and stir well.

3. Blend gelatin and water in a small saucepan, then dissolve over low heat.

4. Add gelatin to hot mixture and stir.

Clotted Cream

1 gallon full-fat milk

1. Let the milk stand overnight in a large pot.

2. Heat and let simmer for an hour, but do not boil.

3. Remove from heat and place the pot in the fridge or a cold room, being careful not to disturb the "skin" forming on top.

4. Let cool for 12 hours, then skim the clotted cream from the top with a wide knife and serve as a spread for scones or toast.

Jam-and-Syrup Tarts

¾ cup all-purpose flour
½ cup softened butter
Jam or marmalade
Pinch of salt
Cold water

1. Preheat oven to 450 degrees F.

2. Sift flour and salt together and cut in soft butter until smooth.

3. Mix in just enough cold water to make a stiff dough and roll out to approximately ¼-inch thickness. Using a cutter or teacup, cut into 3-inch rounds.

4. Fit the cut rounds into individual tart pans ("patty tins") without too much fussing or stretching. Prick the bottom of each tart with a fork so they'll stay flat during baking.

5. Put a small amount of jam or marmalade on top of each but avoid overfilling.

6. Bake for about 15 minutes or until the jam is bubbling and the edges are turning golden.

Empress Scones

Serve warm but not hot with whipped cream on the side.

4¼ cups flour
½ cup (1 stick), plus 1 teaspoon butter
½ cup sugar, plus 2 teaspoons
1 tablespoon baking powder
3 eggs, plus 1 yolk for washing tops
¾ cup dark or golden raisins
1 cup whipping cream

1. Preheat to 350 degrees F.

2. Combine flour, sugar, baking powder, and salt.

3. Whisk and slowly add eggs.

4. Slowly add cream and mix until you have a soft, smooth dough.

5. Roll out dough to ½-inch thickness and cut out shapes of your choice. (You should get about eighteen pieces.)

6. Brush each scone with egg yolk and bake for 25-30 minutes until golden.

Brandy Snaps

Carol, who happens to be English, insisted we include her favorite cookie recipe.

¼ cup butter (I prefer salted but sweet works just as well,
    plus a little for greasing the baking sheet)
¼ cup white sugar
2 tablespoons golden syrup (see recipe below—or, if pressed for time,
    substitute dark corn syrup)
¼ cup all-purpose flour
¼ teaspoon fresh ginger, ground
1 teaspoon brandy
¼ teaspoon lemon zest
Whipped cream (fresh is best, but store-bought works)

1. Preheat oven to 350 degrees F.

2. Melt butter, sugar, and syrup (see recipe below) in a saucepan over low heat so as not to burn.

3. Remove from heat and add the remaining ingredients, with the exception of the whipped cream, and mix well.

4. Drop by teaspoonfuls onto a greased cookie sheet 3 inches apart and bake for 7-10 minutes until golden brown.

5. While the cookies are baking, grease 2 wooden spoon handles and have a wire cooling rack ready.

6. Remove cookies from the oven and allow to rest for a minute or two—but not until they harden.

7. Using a sharp-edged spatula, remove the snaps from the tray and roll each one around one of the greased spoons. When they are fairly cool, carefully slip them off the spoon and place them on the rack to set fully.

8. Once they've cooled, pipe the whipped cream into both ends.

Golden Syrup

This makes more than you'll use for the snaps, but it keeps well in the refrigerator.

½ cup plus 2¼ cups sugar
¼ cup water
1½ cups boiling water
1 tablespoon lemon juice

1. Heat ½ cup sugar and water in a saucepan over low heat until the sugar has dissolved. Turn temperature to low and caramelize for about 8 minutes.

2. Once the mixture is golden amber, add the remaining sugar and slowly drizzle in the boiling water and lemon juice.

3. Stir continuously to combine all the ingredients into a lovely golden-smooth caramel, and simmer for about 15 more minutes until thickened.

4. Remove from heat and cool thoroughly, then transfer to a container and store at room temperature.

Eccles Cakes

This small cake is an English culinary institution dating back hundreds of years. Often baked for general merriment and religious celebrations, they were banned during the strict Puritan reign of the 1600s. They were baked in secret until the ban on festivals was officially lifted in the 1800s.

Be mindful that if you heat them in the microwave, they may spark because of the copious amount of sugar sprinkled on top.

1¾ cups flour
2¼ teaspoons baking powder
1 tablespoon sugar, plus 2 tablespoons
¼ teaspoon salt
¼ cup butter, plus extra for filling
2 eggs, beaten
⅓ cup half-and-half
2 tablespoons raisins
Pinch of cinnamon

1. Preheat the oven to 450 F.

2. Mix together flour, baking powder, 1 tablespoon sugar, and salt.

3. Cut in ¼ cup butter until the mixture is a fine crumble.

4. Set aside 2 tablespoons of the beaten egg and mix what remains with the half-and-half.

5. Make a well in the flour mixture and add egg and half-and-half mixture, then mix to form dough.

6. Roll dough to ¾-inch thickness, then use a cutter to make 2½-inch rounds.

7. Place the rounds on a baking sheet 2 inches apart and poke a hole in the middle of each.

8. Fill rounds with 1 tablespoon raisins and an extra pat of butter.

9. Bring the edges of the rounds up around the filling and pinch together to close, then brush with the reserved egg.

10. Mix 2 tablespoons sugar and cinnamon and sprinkle on top of each cake.

11. Bake for 10-12 minutes or until golden.

Ginger Parkin

This confection originated in Northern England, but today it is popular the world over. Traditionally, it starts out as a hard cake that is stored in a sealed tin or box for several days, where it takes on the softer texture it is meant to have.

¾ cup whole-wheat flour
¾ cup oatmeal
1 teaspoon allspice
1 teaspoon ground ginger
1 teaspoon cinnamon
1 teaspoon cream of tartar
½ teaspoon baking soda
½ cup (1 stick) butter
6 tablespoons brown sugar
¾ cup corn syrup
1 egg, lightly beaten
Candied ginger for garnish

1. Preheat the oven to 300 degrees F.

2. Grease an 8 x 8-inch baking pan.

3. In a mixing bowl, combine all the dry ingredients.

4. Add the butter and blend until crumbly.

5. In a small saucepan, heat the syrup and sugar on low. Remove from heat before the mixture boils, add it to the dry ingredients, then fold in egg and mix well.

6. Pour batter into greased baking pan and bake for 1 hour. Test, and if the center is still wet, bake for another 5-10 minutes.

7. Turn onto a wire rack. When thoroughly cool, cut into 1-inch squares and garnish each square with a piece of ginger.

Almond Shortbread

½ cup (1 stick) butter
½ cup all-purpose flour
¼ cup sugar
¼ cup plus a tad more almonds
¼ teaspoon salt

1. Preheat the oven to 350 degrees F.

2. Grease a 9 x 13-inch baking pan.

3. Cream the butter, then, working with your hands, add it to the dry ingredients until well combined.

4. Transfer the mixture to the baking pan and, working with your knuckles, spread evenly to all corners. Prick all over with a fork.

5. Bake for 45 minutes until light golden brown.

6. While cooling, cut into cookie-sized pieces—but leave them in the pan until completely cool or they will crumble.

Choux Pastry

Choux pastry is a lovely base for making cream puff or profiterole shells, eclairs, or any number of delicious desserts. One of the best things about it is that you need only five basic ingredients and ten minutes to prepare.

4 large eggs, brought to room temperature
½ cup unsalted butter, cut into pieces
1 cup all-purpose flour
½ cup whole milk (or substitute 2 percent)
¼ teaspoon salt

1. Combine and quickly heat the milk, butter, and salt in a saucepan. You want to scald the mixture but not allow it to boil. Reduce the heat, add the flour, and, using a wooden spoon, form into a dough.

2. Remove the dough from the heat and let cool before adding the eggs. (If you add the eggs before the dough has cooled, they'll cook, and you'll end up with a scrambled egg-type mess.) The dough should be warm when you add the room-temperature eggs.

3. Working quickly with the wooden spoon, mix in the eggs until all are incorporated into the dough.

You now have the staple ingredient for many beautiful and tasty sweets for your next afternoon tea. Perhaps, starting with the following.

Tea Puffs

Choux pastry (Use the recipe above or make it from a store-bought mix.)
2 eggs (for egg wash)
Coarse sugar (colored sugar is festive)
Chopped almonds
Whipped cream

1. Preheat the oven to 375 degrees F.

2. Grease a baking sheet with butter.

3. Pipe small balls of choux pastry onto baking sheet, then brush lightly with egg wash.

4. Bake for 30 minutes until puffs are lightly browned, then sprinkle with coarse sugar and chopped almonds and return to the oven for an extra minute or two.

5. If you wish, once the puffs are cool, slice their tops off, add a dollop of whipped cream, and replace the tops.

Madeleines

I had never tasted a madeleine quite like this before my friend Beverly demonstrated this recipe, and they really are special. Those English girls sure know how to get all the goodies on one cookie.

½ cup (1 stick) butter
½ cup sugar
2 eggs, lightly beaten
½ cup flour
A few tablespoons of jam
¼ cup coconut (optional)
¼ cup chopped nuts (optional)
12 maraschino cherries (optional)

1. Preheat the oven to 400 degrees F.

2. Grease 12 madeleine molds.

3. Mix butter and sugar together, then gradually add eggs alternating with flour until thoroughly combined.

4. Fill molds ¾ of the way and bake for about 20 minutes until golden brown and cake-like.

5. When cool, brush each madeleine with melted jam, then roll in coconut and/ or chopped nuts.

6. Brush a bit of jam onto each cherry and stick it on top of the cookie.

Sally Lunn Cake

The origin of this treat is a bit fuzzy. One theory places the cakes in Bath, England, in the late 1770s, being sold by a street vendor named Sally Lunn. A more plausible theory puts the cakes in France as a rich breakfast cake called Solimene (roughly translated as "sun and moon" because of the contrasting dark crust and white center). Whether it has English or French roots, this bakery staple has been adopted by the English as their own. The mixture can be baked in a tube pan as the following recipe calls for or as individual rolls.

1 cup milk, heated
½ cup (1 stick) butter
⅓ cup sugar
1 teaspoon salt
1 tablespoon dry yeast
3½ cups warm water
3 eggs
3½ cups flour

1. Preheat the oven to 425 degrees F.

2. Grease a tube pan.

3. Mix hot milk, butter, sugar, and salt in a large bowl and allow to cool.

4. Stir yeast into warm water and let stand for 5 minutes until dissolved.

5. Add yeast and eggs to the first mixture and mix well, gradually adding in flour.

6. Cover and let rise until doubled in size.

7. Place dough in greased tube pan and bake for 50 minutes.

8. Remove from oven and let cool before cutting.

Dundee Cake

½ cup sultanas (raisins can be substituted)

½ cup currants

¼ cup candied orange peel

¼ cup almonds, plus another ½ ounce for garnish

1⅛ cup all-purpose flour

¼ teaspoon salt

½ teaspoon baking powder

¾ cup (1½ stick) butter

¾ cup sugar

3 eggs

A splash of whole milk

1. Preheat the oven to 350 degrees F.

2. Grease a deep cake pan.

3. Chop sultanas, currants, orange peel, and almonds into bite-size bits.

4. Sift flour, salt, and baking powder together, then stir in fruits and 2 ounces of the nuts.

5. In another bowl, cream the butter and sugar and add in each egg separately.

Recipe continues

6. Combine the wet mixture with the dry, adding milk as necessary to make a thick batter.

7. Pour batter into cake pan and sprinkle the top with ½ ounce almonds.

8. Bake for 1½-2 hours until toothpick inserted comes out clean.

Strawberry Pavlova

Margaret Breskal—darling Denise's mom, who still resides in England—graciously shared her celebrated dessert—one of my all-time favorite treats. She cautions that the eggs must be brought to room temperature before starting and suggests you avoid plastic mixing bowls in favor of glass or crockery.

FOR THE MERINGUE:
1 teaspoon vinegar
6 egg whites, brought to room temperature
1 tablespoon cornstarch
1½ cup finely granulated sugar
1 teaspoon vanilla

FOR THE TOPPING:
3 cups strawberries
1 tablespoon powdered sugar
1½ cups heavy cream
Mint leaves, thin lemon slices (optional)

1. Preheat oven to 250 degrees F.

2. Cut some baking parchment into an oval shape to fit a baking sheet.

3. In a mixer, whisk the egg whites until they form stiff peaks, then gradually add the sugar a little at a time until the mixture looks glossy.

4. Whisk in vanilla, cornstarch, and vinegar.

5. Using a spatula, spread the mixture onto the oval parchment, making sure the outer edge is slightly higher than the center.

6. Bake for 1 hour.

7. Turn off oven but let the meringue sit inside until completely cool: 1½-2 hours.

8. Slice the strawberries and put to one side.

9. Whip the cream with the powdered sugar until firm peaks form.

10. Take the meringue out of the oven and spread the whipped cream over it, then place strawberries on top.

11. If you wish, garnish with mint leaves, thin lemon slices, or even red currant berries for a festive holiday touch.

A Final Word . . .

Tea—and afternoon tea in particular—is a small pleasure but an unparalleled one. Wars have been waged, royal marriages arranged, companies formed, and world problems solved over that perfect cup of tea. It's neither inebriating nor expensive nor fattening, and yet there's nothing quite so effective for regaining one's equilibrium and perspective—or simply relaxing. I can't deny it; I wrote this book to extol the pleasures of my own habit in the hope of drawing others into it. Having indulged me with your attention throughout these pages, I hope you'll reward yourself with a bewitching cup of your favorite brew.

Cheers!

Photo Credits

Cover Photo: Michael Lee Stever

Title Page & Chapter Openers: "Vintage Tea Cup stock photo" by PILIPIPA https://www.istockphoto.com/photo/vintage-tea-cup-gm660644100-120457403?clarity=false

Page X: "Vintage Tea Cups stock photo" by PILIPIPA https://www.istockphoto.com/photo/vintage-tea-cups-gm660644112-120457409?clarity=false

Page 3 "Ancient China. Oriental people. Tea ceremony. Traditional Chinese paintings. Tradition and culture of Asia. Classic wall drawing. Murals and watercolor asian style. Hand-drawn vector illustration" by matrioshka https://www.shutterstock.com/image-vector/ancient-china-oriental-people-tea-ceremony-1751049509

Page 5 "Porcelain teapot in classic style on white stock photo" by ShushanHarutyunyan https://www.istockphoto.com/photo/porcelain-teapot-in-classic-style-on-white-gm486254814-72438379?clarity=false

Page 8 "Pretty pink and gold vintage teapot and teacups - tea party" by Alison Henley https://www.shutterstock.com/image-photo/pretty-pink-gold-vintage-teapot-teacups-670737223

Page 10 "Close-up picture of a farmer's hand picking tea leaf from the tree and put in a bamboo basket at tea plantation in Chiangmai province northern of Thailand. Organic Natural selected by picker." by skipper_sr https://www.shutterstock.com/image-photo/close-picture-farmers-hand-picking-tea-1830706922

Page 13 "Vector infographics with illustrations of tea processing. Authentic tea production hand sketched scheme." by Vlada Young https://www.shutterstock.com/image-vector/vector-infographics-illustrations-tea-processing-authentic-627583913

Page 15 "various types of tea: hibiscus, oolong, sencha, black, green, herbal tea on a white background, a collection of tea leaves" by Leka Sergeeva https://www.shutterstock.com/image-photo/various-types-tea-hibiscus-oolong-sencha-1748288174

Page 16 "Tea pours into a cup with lemon from teapot" by Dmitry Elagin https://www.shutterstock.com/image-photo/tea-pours-into-cup-lemon-teapot-93780715

Page 19 "Afternoon tea set stock photo" by Peter Cernoch https://www.istockphoto.com/photo/afternoon-tea-set-gm653261568-122726389?clarity=false

Page 22 "Tea being poured into a cup on a table set for afternoon tea stock photo" by SergioZacchi https://www.istockphoto.com/photo/tea-being-poured-into-a-cup-on-a-table-set-for-afternoon-tea-gm471634556-62895524?clarity=false

Page 25 "Classic tea time. stock photo" by martinedoucet https://www.istockphoto.com/photo/classic-tea-time-gm154946417-15765534?clarity=false

Page 26 "Beautiful little girl and her grandmother having a tea party stock photo" by geniebird https://www.istockphoto.com/photo/beautiful-little-girl-and-her-grandmother-having-a-tea-party-gm134445492-18117522?clarity=false

Page 28 "Traditional high tea menu. A set selection of finger sandwiches, petit fours, sweet and savory pastries, scone with preserve and clotted cream, tea, or coffee." by Andri Andiansyah https://www.shutterstock.com/image-photo/traditional-high-tea-menu-set-selection-1898748127

Page 30 "Almond flake on cake stock photo" by jreika https://www.istockphoto.com/photo/almond-flake-on-cake-gm626397232-110590433?clarity=false

Page 32: "Tea strainer" by Igor Kovalchuk https://stock.adobe.com/images/tea-strainer/39009858

Page 34: "tea and milk" by GVictoria

https://stock.adobe.com/images/tea-and-milk/419738

Page 37 "portrait of a beautiful woman dressed in Baroque style, drinking tea and looking away. photo for the cover of a historical romance novel" by Lemalisa https://www.shutterstock.com/image-photo/portrait-beautiful-woman-dressed-baroque-style-1831616377

Page 38 "scones on a white plate, a jar of strawberry jam and a cup of tea on a gray background" by natashamam https://www.shutterstock.com/image-photo/scones-on-white-plate-jar-strawberry-1612970593

Page 39 "Afternoon tea" by Ruth Black https://www.shutterstock.com/image-photo/afternoon-tea-150925592

Page 41 "Pretty Pastel Tea Cups in Row - Afternoon Tea Party" by Alison Henley https://www.shutterstock.com/image-photo/pretty-pastel-tea-cups-row-afternoon-608495408

Page 44 "fresh homemade scones with clotted cream and jam" by Pierre Molle https://www.shutterstock.com/image-photo/fresh-homemade-scones-clotted-cream-jam-1686571564

Page 45 "tea bags and loose green tea on a white background" by Pavel Andreyenka https://www.shutterstock.com/image-photo/tea-bags-loose-green-on-white-404503543

Page 48 Courtesy of Michael Lee Stever

Page 51 Courtesy of Frank Vlastnik

Page 54 Provided by the author from her personal collection

Page 56 Provided by the author from her personal collection

Page 59 Provided by the author from her personal collection

Page 62 "East 64th Street, Manhattan, New York, USA - April 21, 2020. Alice's Tea Cup Chapter II - New York City's most whimsical tea house." by Maya K. Photography https://www.shutterstock.com/image-photo/east-64th-street-manhattan-new-york-2149167005

Page 63 "New York, New York, USA - January 10, 2020: This awning is located on Alice's Tea Cup chapter two off Lexington Avenue in Manhattan." by DW labs Incorporated https://www.shutterstock.com/image-photo/new-york-usa-january-10-2020-1613980333

Page 67 Provided by the author from her personal collection

Page 70 Provided by the author from her personal collection

Page 72 Courtesy of The Tea House on Los Rios

Page 73 Courtesy of The Tea House on Los Rios

ABOUT THE AUTHOR

LADY PATRICIA FARMER is a historian, best-selling author, businesswoman, and former model. She's been fascinated with the glamour, magic, and history of New York City's quintessential Plaza Hotel ever since the day her mother introduced her to the ritual of afternoon tea at the hotel's Palm Court when she was just seven years old. She continues her in-depth research uncovering all the secrets and history this mythical, landmark hotel holds. Lady Patricia has followed the entertainment industry as an insider, and archivist all her life. Her work draws upon a lifetime of close friendships and socializing among personalities and celebrities around the world and has spent the last decade writing about some of our most significant cultural institutions.